The Garden in My Mind

ACTIVITY GUIDE

Lessons for social skill and common core development

Classroom ideas for teaching the skills of ignoring distractions from others and making positive choices

Written by
Stephie McCumbee, M.Ed., NBCT
Illustrated by
Lisa M. Griffin

BOYS TOWN Press
Boys Town, Nebraska

The Garden in My Mind Activity Guide

ISBN 978-1-934490-55-6

Published by Boys Town Press
14100 Crawford St.
Boys Town, Nebraska 68010

Cover and Inside Page Design: Anne Hughes

Printed in the United States
10 9 8 7 6 5 4 3 2 1

For a Boys Town Press catalog, call 1-800-282-6657
or visit our website: BoysTownPress.org

BOYS TOWN
Saving Children Healing Families

Boys Town Press is the publishing division of Boys Town, a national organization serving children and families.

A Note from the Author

As the teacher of fourth-grade gifted students, I understand the importance of working smarter, not harder. This book includes everything you need to help your little friends learn how to make good choices and avoid distractions.

This book is organized in three sections:

1. Lesson plans to teach students how to avoid distractions and make positive choices
2. Activities that use *The Garden in My Mind* story to teach Common Core Standards
3. Explanation of a behavior-management system that focuses on the theme of gardening

In addition, these activities are organized according to **Revised Bloom's Taxonomy.** Each activity is coded using stars.

Remembering

Applying

Evaluating

Understanding

Analyzing

Creating

A Note for Parents

TEACHER NOTE: You can print this letter off the enclosed CD, and send home to your students' parents.

Dear Parents and Caring Adults,

The classroom setting is always evolving. Now, with classes often averaging 25 students, it is increasingly important that you speak with your children about how to avoid distractions and make positive choices. Both of these behavioral skills will help your child have a successful school year and can be generalized to other situations in life. Below are some tips to help ensure that your child knows how to avoid distractions and make positive choices.

Help your child understand that while having a best friend in school is a good thing, sitting next to that friend, who might want to talk or play during class, is not a good idea. Analyze the situation together. Discuss why it might be a better idea for your child to sit next to a student who is not his or her best friend.

Practice building your child's "stamina." For example, set up a chart that records the number of minutes your child can stay focused, even when there are distractions. Reward your child when he or she reaches benchmarks.

Discuss with your child how some students like the negative attention they get when they distract others. Teach him or her how to avoid that trap by not making eye contact with or laughing at the disruptive student.

Teach your child to make positive, informed decisions by using a "think aloud" model. This means "thinking verbally" by saying aloud the choices your child should make in his or her life. When it comes to making good choices, have your child think carefully about the choice that is to be made. Together, consider all options and weigh the outcomes.

TEACHER SIGNATURE DATE

Notes to Educators

The first few weeks of school are the most important days to establish classroom expectations. Distractions in the classroom prohibit students from learning and can lead to a year of behavior referrals. It is best to set clear expectations on the first day of school and reinforce these skills throughout the year.

The goal of this teacher's guide is to help students explicitly learn what distracting behaviors look like, how to deal with distractions by others, and how to generalize these tips outside the classroom.

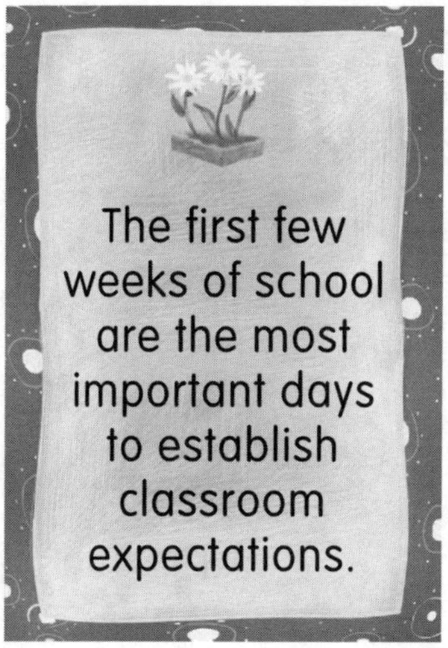

Begin by introducing to the class the Skill of Ignoring Distractions from Others.

Ask students to "quick write" about a time when they were distracted by someone in class. Once students are finished, have them "turn and talk" about the experience. Ask several students to share how the distractions affected them.

Then, introduce the title of the book, *The Garden in My Mind*, and have students predict what the story is about. Take a picture walk of the book and have students make predictions. After the picture walk, read the book aloud to the class.

After you have read the story, ask students to recall the tips Maci's mom gave her to help her ignore distracting behaviors. Have each student create a poster using these steps and display the posters in the classroom or throughout the school.

Teaching Social Skill Sheets

Name: ______________________________ Date: ____________________

Predict the Truth

DIRECTIONS: Before you read *The Garden in My Mind,* look at each statement and choose whether it is true or false. Circle your answer in the left-hand column. After you read the story, look at each statement again and decide if it is true or false. Circle your answer in the right-hand column.

BEFORE READING	STATEMENT	AFTER READING
True or False	If someone is trying to distract you, you should make eye contact with him or her.	*True or False*
True or False	If someone is playing and being silly in class, you should respond by telling another student.	*True or False*
True or False	It is okay to tell the teacher if someone is distracting you.	*True or False*
True or False	Choosing to sit beside your friend in class is always a good idea.	*True or False*
True or False	If you are trying to make a choice, it is best to think about the positive and negative consequences of the choice.	*True or False*
True or False	If someone is distracting you, he or she is probably distracting other students in the classroom.	*True or False*
True or False	Some students will always make bad choices, and they can't help it.	*True or False*

SKILL

Ignoring Distractions from Others

Practice the Skill

Choose one or more of the following activities to help reinforce the Skill of Ignoring Distractions from Others:

1. Have students work in groups of three or four to create skits where the students act out the appropriate ways to avoid distracting behaviors.

2. Have students work in pairs to create a rap that teaches them how to ignore distractions from others.

3. Have students create a play whose characters have to use the tips to avoid someone who is distracting them, either in class or at home.

4. Have students write a poem in which the main character has to teach his or her friend how to ignore distractions.

Reinforce the Skill

Hold students accountable for meeting the expectations you have set throughout the year. *Reward positive behavior!*

Putting It Into Practice

Avoiding Distractions

Teacher Instructions

1. Read *The Garden in My Mind* to your students.
2. Discuss the tips Maci used in the story.
3. Tell students that throughout the year, you will be monitoring them closely to see who is practicing these tips in their everyday life.
4. Later in the day, plan a silent reading time. Allow students to read silently around the room. Use this time to make notes about sounds, movement, playing, fake reading, and any other important observations.
5. Call students back together to have a discussion. Ask students to share what distractions they noticed during silent reading time. Then discuss your observations. The accountability will go a long way.
6. Continue to do this periodically through the year. Reward students who are doing the right thing with a reward coupon.

Want to do this activity with K-2 students?

With younger students, watch them during calendar time or during your morning meeting. Record behaviors that are both positive and negative. Discuss your observations at the end of your meeting. Later in the day, pull aside students who were not making positive decisions and discuss what you saw and how they could have made better choices.

Name: ______________________________ Date: ______________

Self-Interview (GRADES 3-5)

Think about a time when you distracted someone from learning. Explain what you were doing and how you know it was distracting to others. ______________________________

____

____

____

____

Explain what you should have done differently. ______________________________

____

____

____

____

Explain what you learned from the experience. ______________________________

____

____

____

____

How can you help your friends learn the importance of avoiding distractions? ______________

____

____

____

STUDENT WORKSHEET

Name: ______________________________ Date: ______________

My Graphic Novel (GRADES K-2)

DIRECTIONS: Use the boxes below to create a comic strip for *The Garden in My Mind.* Pretend that you are the author, and you have decided to continue the story. Draw an alternate ending and label your pictures.

Name: ______________________________ Date: ______________

My Novel (GRADES 3-5)

DIRECTIONS: Pretend that you are the book's author, and you have decided to continue the story. Create an alternate ending that begins with Maci telling Trey about the "special tips."

Create A Skit (GRADES 3-5)

OBJECTIVE:

This activity is designed to help students practice using the skills taught in the book.

Teacher Instructions

1. Divide students into groups of three or four.
2. Have students create a skit whose characters face some sort of distraction. In the skit, the characters must use only one of the tips to help them avoid the distraction.
3. Have groups perform their skits for the class.
4. Have students in the "audience" guess which tip the actors in the skit used to avoid the distraction.

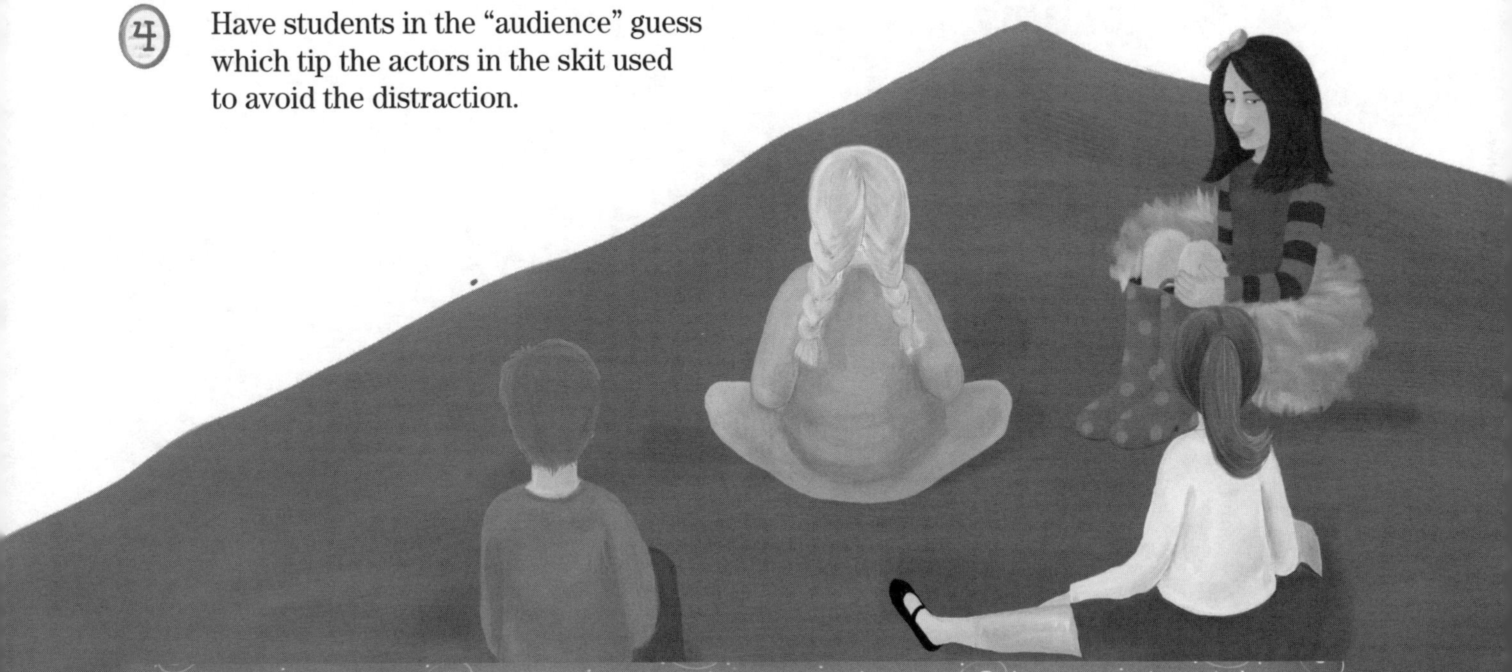

Want to do this activity with K-2 students?

K – Act out different situations in which you are making negative choices. Have students say what you should have done to avoid making negative choices.

Grades 1-2 – Create a list of possible distractions within the classroom. Write them on index cards (one per card). Have students draw a card, then create and perform a skit about ignoring the distraction written on the card.

Gardening 101

Maci's Tips

Give your full attention to the task you are doing.

Refocus yourself if distractions are brewing.

Observe "gardeners" whose good choices help their gardens grow.

Work together to create your best flower show.

STUDENT WORKSHEET

Name: ______________________________ Date: ______________

Justify Your Thinking

DIRECTIONS: Use Maci's Tips and prioritize them from most important (1) to least important (4).

1

2

3

4

Defend why you believe these tips are in the best order. ______________________________

____

____

____

Want to do this activity with K-2 students?

With younger students, have them choose the one tip they think is most important. Then have them write the reason they chose that tip.

Grouping Distractions

OBJECTIVE:

This activity is designed to teach students to be aware of behaviors that are distracting.

Materials Needed

- Lined paper
- Markers
- Poster paper
- Clock
- Pencils
- White board

Teacher Instructions

Have students sit in groups of four. Give each group one poster paper, a sheet of lined paper, markers, and a pencil.

1. Have students work in groups to brainstorm behaviors in their world (classroom or home) that are distracting. Students should record all their ideas on the lined paper. (15 minutes)

2. After students have brainstormed as many behaviors as possible, have the groups share their answers with the class while you record them on the white board. Do not record answers that have already been stated.

3. Have groups use their poster paper to identify and group together distractions that are similar, and then label them. For example, nails on a chalkboard, tapping, and humming could be grouped together and labeled as "Distracting Sounds."

Want to do this activity with K-2 students?

Have students call out distractions they see in the classroom. As they are speaking, record their thoughts on the board. Together as a class, put words into possible categories based on where each distraction might be seen.

You've Been Hired (GRADES 3-5)

OBJECTIVE:
This activity is designed to help students learn how to ignore distractions from others. *This activity addresses the plan/organize Executive Function.*

Materials Needed

- Markers
- Crayons
- Construction paper
- A copy of *The Garden in My Mind*
- "You've Been Hired Checklist" student worksheet
- "Pamphlet Template" (optional)

Teacher Instructions

1. Read *The Garden in My Mind* and discuss the tips that Maci's mom told Maci to use to avoid Trey's distractions.

2. Tell the students they have recently been hired to create a pamphlet for schools to use.

3. Pass out the checklist sheet to students and go over the requirements for the pamphlet project:
   - The pamphlet should include tips for avoiding distractions, a slogan to reinforce the skills, possible things that might be distracting to others, and illustrations.
   - Discuss with students how to use the "You've Been Hired Checklist" to organize their planning.
   - You may decide to pass out the "Pamphlet Template" for students to use in their activity. (optional)

4. Once students have completed their pamphlets, have them move around the classroom to view everyone's pamphlets.

Name: ______________________________ Date: __________________

You've Been Hired Checklist

DIRECTIONS: As you are working on your pamphlet, check off each item as you complete it.

- ☐ I have read *The Garden in My Mind* and understand the main idea.
- ☐ I have folded my construction paper in half and made a pamphlet.
- ☐ My pamphlet includes tips for avoiding distractions.
- ☐ My pamphlet includes a catchy slogan to help others avoid distractions.
- ☐ My pamphlet discusses possible distractions that occur in the classroom.
- ☐ My pamphlet includes possible distractions outside the classroom.
- ☐ My pamphlet has illustrations.

Slogan

Avoiding Distractions Tips

Classroom Distractions

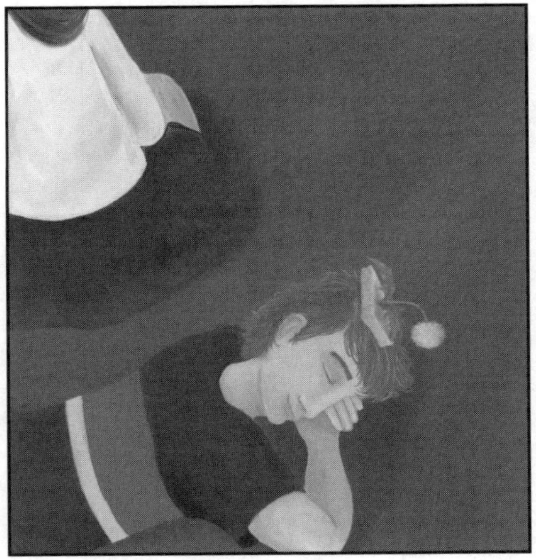

Other Distractions

fold

fold

Name: ______________________________ Date: ______________

Dear Trey (GRADES 3-5)

DIRECTIONS: Pretend you are Mrs. Julian. Write a letter to Trey Thompson explaining how the choices he made affected him. Include the future consequences that might occur if his behavior continues. Then, give Trey strategies that will help him begin to make better choices.

Teaching Language Skill Sheets

Name: ______________________________ Date: ____________________

Timeline (GRADES 3-5)

DIRECTIONS: Read *The Garden in My Mind*, then create a timeline for the events as they happened in the story.

FINISH

START

SAMPLE

Name: ______________________________ Date: ____________________

Timeline (GRADES 3-5)

DIRECTIONS: Read *The Garden in My Mind*, then create a timeline for the events as they happened in the story.

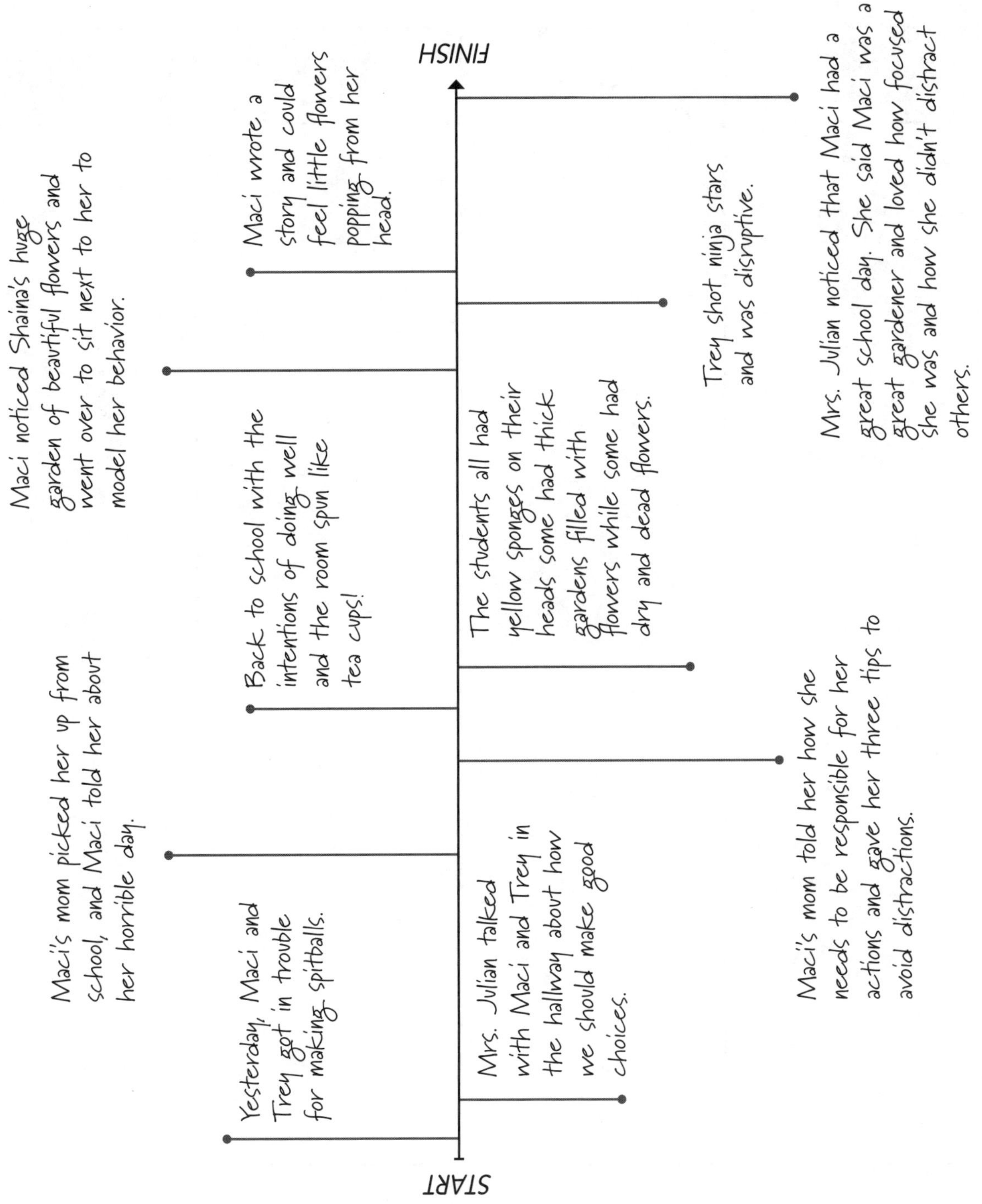

Name: ______________________________ Date: ____________________

Draw the Story (GRADES K-2)

DIRECTIONS: List the transition words you found in the story to show the sequence of events over time. Then, draw pictures of the main events in the story.

First	Next	Then	Last

Name: ______________________ Date: ______________

Preview - Before Reading

What is the title of the text?	Look at the cover and make a prediction.

Look at the back jacket of the book and make a prediction.	Do a "picture walk" of the book and make a prediction about what you think will happen.

List any thoughts you have before reading the book.	Make one connection with the book before you begin reading it.

What do you already know about the topic?	What might happen in the story? What might you learn about?

Name: ________________________ Date: ____________

Sentence Starter

1. Read the story.

2. Complete the sentence starters below:

Who: ________________________

____

What: ________________________

____

When: ________________________

____

Where: ________________________

____

Why: ________________________

____

How: ________________________

____

3. Write a short summary that includes the stems above: ________________________

____

____

____

____

Name: ______________________________ Date: ________________

Story Element Word List

DIRECTIONS: Look at the following list of words. Write each word in the column where you think it fits best on the "Story Element Sheet."

Ryeleigh	hall	playing
focus	Shaina	yesterday
rock, paper, scissors	eye contact	ignore
grub worm	ninja stars	Maci
school	disappointed	screeching
mom	Aunt Te Te	floor
Mrs. Parker	playing	science class
Trey	Mrs. Julian	sprawled
moment	Chia pet	wither
fade	scrunched	grumbled

Name: ______________________________ Date: ______________

Story Element Sheet

DIRECTIONS: Look at the "Story Element Word List." Write each word in the column where you think it fits best.

Character	Setting	Problem	Solution

Name: ______________________________ Date: ________________

My Understanding

DIRECTIONS: While reading *The Garden in My Mind,* identify and write down in the left-hand column three main points of the story that made you think. Record your thoughts about the story in the "My Reaction" column. Remember, good readers make connections and predictions as well as visualize and summarize while they read.

What the Story Says	My Reaction
"Trey sprawled out on the carpet—belly first, like one of those polar bear rugs I've seen on TV."	I was able to visualize what Trey looked liked because I have seen a polar bear rug before.

Name: ______________________ Date: ______________

Compare and Contrast Diagram

DIRECTIONS: Compare and contrast the story's main characters. Write down the things the characters have in common in the overlapping parts of their circles. The things that are different about the characters should go in the outer parts of their circles.

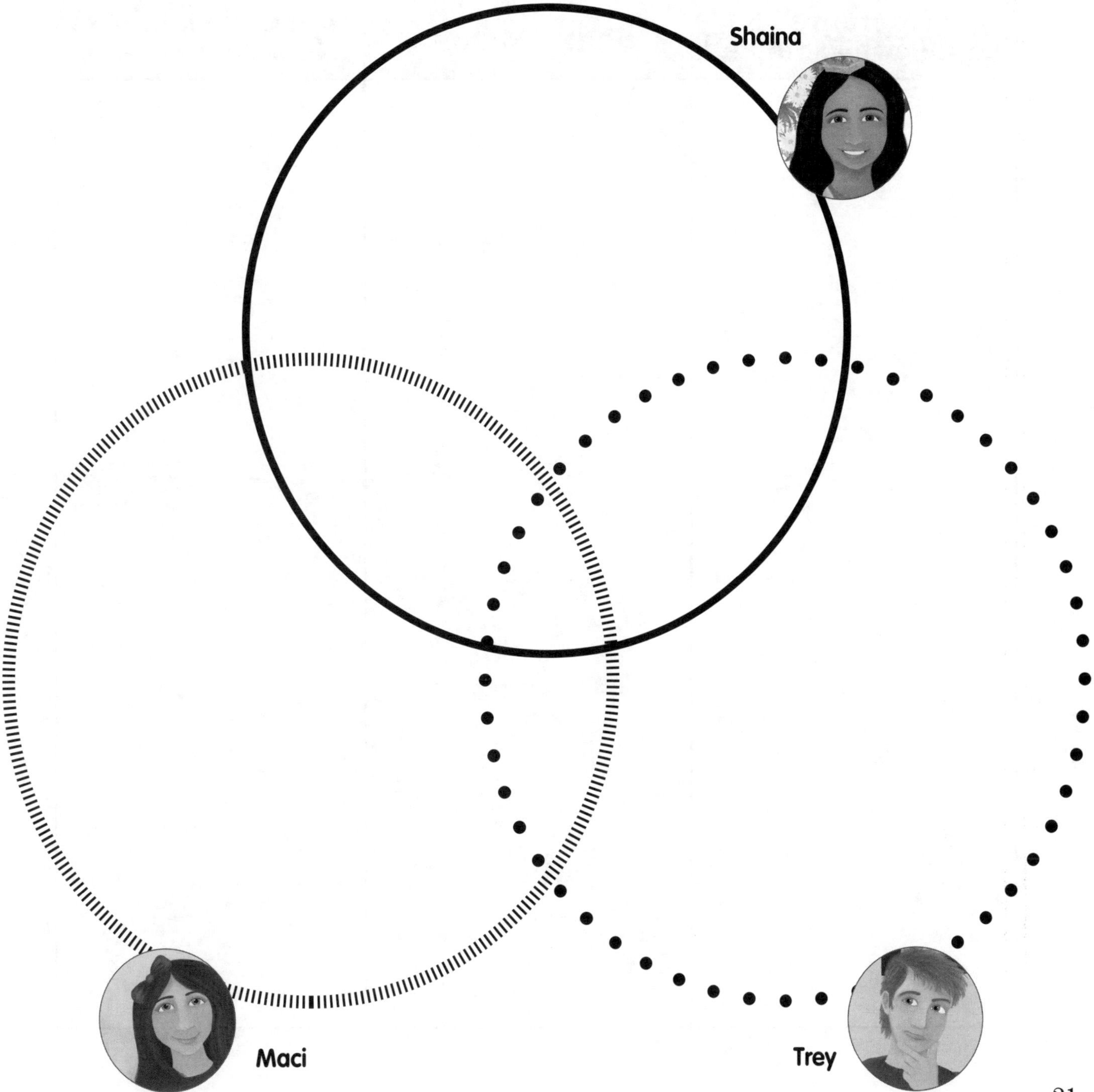

Name: ______________________ Date: ____________

On the Hunt: Figurative Language

DIRECTIONS: The author uses many different examples of figurative language. With a partner, identify examples of figurative language. Then, complete the chart based on the information you find.

Figurative Language Example	What it Means	Name of Figurative Language Used

Name: ______________________________ Date: ____________________

On the Hunt: Main Ideas

DIRECTIONS: Determine two or more main ideas of the story and explain how they are supported by key details in the story.

	Main Idea One: ________________ ________________	**Main Idea Two:** ________________ ________________
Supporting Detail 1:		
Supporting Detail 2:		
Supporting Detail 3:		
Supporting Detail 4:		

Compose a Song

OBJECTIVE:
Students will compose a song that teaches other students how to avoid distractions from others and make positive choices. The song should include at least three examples of figurative language. *This activity addresses the managing time and attention Executive Function.*

Teacher Instructions

1. Have students pair up.
2. Give each pair a list of five popular song lyrics to choose from.
3. Students have five minutes to agree on the song they would like to rewrite. Set the timer.
4. Once students have chosen a song, pass out the rubric so they can see what the final product should include. Go over the criteria for this project together.
5. Have students record Maci's Tips (pg. 14) in their journals so they can check them off as they use each one.
6. Students should come up with three sentences that use figurative language to include in their song. (10 Minutes)
7. Give students two 45-minute sessions to rewrite the song. Remind students about the time limit as you monitor them.
8. Once students have completed their song, have each pair present it to the class.
9. Evaluate the students' songs using the rubric on the next page.

Compose a Song

	Score 3	Score 2	Score 1
Content	Song includes at least 5 tips.	Song includes at least 4 tips.	Song includes 3 or fewer tips.
Audience	The audience is highly engaged.	The audience is engaged.	The audience is not engaged.
Purpose	Song highly convinces students to make good choices and includes 3 examples of figurative language.	Song provides several examples that are convincing and includes 2 examples of figurative language.	Song provides few examples that are convincing and includes 1 example of figurative language.
Organization	The student pair is very organized during the presentation.	The student pair is somewhat organized during the presentation.	The student pair lacks organization during the presentation.

Behavior Rewards, Reminders, and Coupons

Behavior System

OBJECTIVE:
This behavior system includes both the positive rewards needed to encourage good choices and the refocusing sheets needed to refocus students.

DIRECTIONS: Read *The Garden in My Mind* to the class.

Materials Needed

- Printed sponge refocusing cards
- Copies of "Refocusing Note Home Sheet"
- Positive behavior management books
- Hole puncher
- Positive behavior management books to place at a "refocusing table"
- Refocusing directions sheet (laminated)
- Flower Seed Packet Punch Card
- Reward Coupons
- Copies of the "Positive Note Home Sheet"

Behavior Management

1. When students are not making positive choices, you can give them a refocusing sponge to warn them of their behavior.

2. If students continue to make negative choices, have them go to a "refocusing table" and complete the "Refocusing Note Home Sheet," which is to be signed by their parents. While students are waiting to speak with you about their choices, they should read one of the books at the station that encourages good behavior, like *The Garden in My Mind*.

Behavior Rewarding

When students model positive behaviors, reward them by punching their flower seed packets. When a student's packet has been punched five times, he or she may choose a reward coupon.

When students struggle to make positive choices, have them complete the "Positive Note Home" sheet and have their parents sign it.

Coupon Examples

Coupon Examples *continued*

Possible Coupon Rewards

DIRECTIONS: Use any of the options from the list below to create your own coupon rewards.

- [ ] Sit at the teacher's desk (1 hour)
- [ ] Change classroom jobs for the day
- [ ] Be the Teacher's Assistant for a day
- [ ] Use the rolling chair (1 hour)
- [ ] Eat with a friend
- [ ] Read to another class
- [ ] Take shoes off during reading time
- [ ] Extra computer time
- [ ] Free iPad time
- [ ] Homework Pass (even numbered days only)
- [ ] Eat lunch with the teacher
- [ ] Go to the treasure chest
- [ ] Receive a note home ("Positive Note Home Sheet")
- [ ] Choose a friend to work with
- [ ] Be the Line Leader for a day
- [ ] Be the Special Helper for a day
- [ ] Show and Tell Coupon
- [ ] Move around the room to complete work (at a book nook or by the bean bag)
- [ ] Eat lunch with someone from another class

Flower Seed Packets Punch Card

DIRECTIONS: Have students turn in their Flower Seed Packet Punch Cards after all ovals are punched (or marked). The five-oval punch card is ideal for kids who need frequent reinforcement (younger students and those struggling with their behaviors). The ten-oval punch card is ideal for kids who need less frequent reinforcement (older students and those with more behavioral skills).

Refocusing Reminders

Teacher Instructions:

1. Mount, cut, and laminate the sponge reminder cards for students from the following page and on CD.

2. Carry the cards with you throughout the day. If you notice someone who could use a little reminder of the tips, quietly hand him or her a "sponge."

This visual reminder allows students to quietly read the tips again and refocus their behavior. It also serves as a visual for you so that you can easily see who you have given warnings to. Consistency with this is very important!

Give your full attention to the task you are doing.

Refocus yourself if distractions are brewing.

Observe "gardeners" whose good choices help their gardens grow.

Work together to create your best flower show.

Quiet Refocusing Reminders

DIRECTIONS: Include the tips on the back of the sponges.

STOP
what you are doing and think about how you can **GROW** your garden!

STOP
what you are doing and think about how you can **GROW** your garden!

STOP
what you are doing and think about how you can **GROW** your garden!

STOP
what you are doing and think about how you can **GROW** your garden!

Quiet Refocusing Reminders *continued*

Maci's Tips

- ★ **G**ive your full attention to the task you are doing.
- ★ **R**efocus yourself if distractions are brewing.
- ★ **O**bserve "gardeners" whose good choices help their gardens grow.
- ★ **W**ork together to create your best flower show.

Maci's Tips

- ★ **G**ive your full attention to the task you are doing.
- ★ **R**efocus yourself if distractions are brewing.
- ★ **O**bserve "gardeners" whose good choices help their gardens grow.
- ★ **W**ork together to create your best flower show.

Maci's Tips

- ★ **G**ive your full attention to the task you are doing.
- ★ **R**efocus yourself if distractions are brewing.
- ★ **O**bserve "gardeners" whose good choices help their gardens grow.
- ★ **W**ork together to create your best flower show.

Maci's Tips

- ★ **G**ive your full attention to the task you are doing.
- ★ **R**efocus yourself if distractions are brewing.
- ★ **O**bserve "gardeners" whose good choices help their gardens grow.
- ★ **W**ork together to create your best flower show.

Monthly Behavior Charts

STUDENT:

Monday	Tuesday	Wednesday	Thursday	Friday

STUDENT:

Monday	Tuesday	Wednesday	Thursday	Friday

Refocusing Directions

1. Think about the choices you made that lead you here.
2. Complete the "Refocusing Note Home Sheet" for your parents.
3. Read silently from one of the books provided until I am able to speak with you about your choices.
4. Remember, tomorrow is a new day and a fresh start to grow your garden.

Refocusing Note Home Sheet

DIRECTIONS: You can print this letter off the enclosed CD, and send it home to your student's parents or guardians.

Dear______________________________,

Today I did not make a positive choice at school. I know this behavior is distracting to my classmates and distracts my own learning. Can we talk about the choices I made and how I should have handled the situation differently so that tomorrow I can make better choices?

Today during class I did not make a good choice when: ______________________________

____

____

After talking with my parents tonight, I learned:

____

____

In the future I will: ______________________________

____

____

____

______________________________		______________________________	
STUDENT SIGNATURE	DATE	PARENT/GUARDIAN SIGNATURE	DATE

Positive Note Home Sheet

DIRECTIONS: You can print this letter off the enclosed CD, and send it home to your student's parents or guardians.

Dear__________________________,

Today I made a positive choice at school. I'm practicing the tips we learned so that I can be sure to stay on task and not distract myself and others.

Today I made a good choice when: ____________

____

____

____

____

____

STUDENT SIGNATURE	DATE	PARENT/GUARDIAN SIGNATURE	DATE